Heartfelt Fundraising

Cover design by: Devon G. Mitchell

ISBN 979-8-90271-502-3 (Paperback)

ISBN 979-8-90271-503-0 (Hardcover)

Library of Congress Control Number: NRC116099

Printed in the United States of America

Publisher Devon G. Mitchell

www.heartfeltfundraising.com

Dedication

This book is dedicated to my family and the community that taught me what leadership truly means.

To my friend Mark, whose journey revealed how fragile life can be, and how powerful preparation, presence, and people can be when it matters most.

To my wife, Samantha, and our children, your love, patience, and belief have been my constant foundation. You stood with me through moments of uncertainty and growth, reminding me that purpose begins at home and leadership is lived long before it is declared.

And to the friends, colleagues, and community members who step forward without being asked, who say yes before they know how, and who remind us that real impact is never achieved alone.

This work exists because of you.
May it encourage others to look within, leverage what already surrounds them, and press the "up" button toward a future shaped by heart, readiness, and shared responsibility.

Forword

What one elevator ride can do, going up

I was waiting for an elevator the first time I met Devon Mitchell. The doors opened and out walked a man with one of the kindest smiles I'd ever seen. He said hello and, instead of getting on the elevator, I returned his greeting and we began a conversation. I don't remember precisely what we talked about. But I do recall that there was something special about this guy that made me want to learn more.

That first meeting took place at an Anytime Fitness annual conference in Palm Springs in 2014. As the National Media Director for the company, I'd had the pleasure of meeting more than a thousand Anytime Fitness gym owners over the years - fitness professionals and entrepreneurs dedicated to improving the lives of others. Devon exemplified the finest characteristics in the best of them - creative, smart, and determined to truly make a difference.

After the conference, we kept in touch and Devon told me about one of the members of his gym (Mark Allen) - and their shared dream to compete internationally together in a duathlon. I secured a little funding from Anytime Fitness to help Devon and Mark realize that dream, but their adventure in Spain turned out to be just the first leg of an amazing journey.

Devon will share with you what happened next, but I'll reveal that a life-and-death moment prompted Devon to reach for even greater heights.

Together with his extraordinary wife, Samantha, their wonderful children, and their large network of friends, Devon committed himself to improving the lives of countless others in his community, saving the lives of people he may never even know.

Nobody accomplishes the sort of things Devon has achieved without a detailed plan. In "*Heartfelt Fundraising*", Devon shares secrets and life lessons to help you realize your own dreams. Whether it's improving public health, increasing access to quality education, helping others find safe places to sleep, or whatever other good things you want to do in the world, Devon's actionable strategies will help you pave the road to success.

From finding your purpose to setting achievable goals and building on little victories, it's all here on these pages. All you need to do is press the "up" button and ride the elevator to new possibilities.

Congratulations! By opening this book, you've taken the first step towards wherever your passion leads you. Now, don't stop until you've reached the finish line.

Table Of Contents

Preface

I never imagined a single moment could alter the course of my life. The phone rang, and the voice on the other end of the line said Mark suffered a cardiac event at his triathlon Race. Silence, questions, tears, and all the emotions you could imagine showed up at the same time. I've never had this feeling in my adult life, so as my body was trying to process the words and handle the sudden overwhelming physical weakness, how do I process this information? I felt the tears running down my face, and then it hit me. The seconds felt like hours; the reality of the situation was that "my friend's life lies in the balance."

Those minutes felt eternal. But against the odds, Mark survived. The person who performed CPR on that kayak saved his life before the paramedics even arrived. Mark's heart was restarted after multiple defibrillator shocks and urgent care. Later, I learned just how lucky he was: nearly

90% of people who suffer cardiac arrest outside of a hospital don't make it. redcross.org. Every minute without CPR drastically reduces the chances of survival. redcross.org. Mark beat those odds because someone nearby was prepared and courageous enough to act. That realization hit me hard. If not for that stranger's knowledge and willingness to help, my friend, a 47-year-old father and husband full of life, would likely have been lost. Mark's recovery was slow but miraculous – from not being able to speak or walk in the days after, to ultimately returning to our gym and even training again five days a week, week anytimefitness.com. His physical Fitness and sheer determination played a crucial role in that recovery, but it all started with prompt CPR and a community coming together around a crisis.

In the aftermath of Mark's cardiac arrest, my perspective on health, community, and purpose fundamentally changed. I had always valued fitness and wellness, from my athletic day as a multiple sports athlete and owning and operating a fitness facility with my wife Samantha, helping others find and stay in their healthy place. But this was different. I had witnessed, in the most visceral way, how a life could hang in the balance and how preparedness and compassion could tip the scales toward hope. The experience ignited a spark within me. I realized that promoting health and wellness wasn't just a profession or business goal; it was a deeply personal mission to save lives and strengthen my community.

A few months later, I was invited to attend the American Heart Association Heart Ball in Philadelphia. This elegant annual gala brings together donors, volunteers, survivors, healthcare professionals and the community in support of the AHA's mission. That evening, Mark was honored on stage as a survivor, to resounding applause. I looked around the grand ballroom filled with hundreds of people dedicated to heart health, like that bystander at the race, had decided to step up for others. The atmosphere was filled with a sense of hope and gratitude. In that moment, I felt the full weight of why organizations like the AHA exist. They were not just hosting a fundraiser; they were celebrating second chances like Mark's and rallying everyone to support a life-saving cause.

As I listened to stories of survivors and the incredible work being done in research and community programs, something clicked, "My ah-ha moment". The American Heart Association's mission aligned with the work we were doing at our facility, and it was unmistakable. Both were about saving and improving lives. Attending the Heart Ball was more than a good evening; it was my call to action. I realized I could no longer remain a passive participant in this fight against heart disease. I had to become an active contributor.

By the end of that night, I made a quiet vow to myself: I would use every resource and ounce of passion I had to support the cause of heart health. I would join the movement, lending my voice and leadership to spread awareness about CPR, healthy living, and heart disease prevention. I wanted to ensure that more families would have stories of survival, resilience, and hope, rather than stories of tragic loss.

This book is the result of that journey and commitment. Heartfelt Fundraising: Mastering Six-Figure Success with Passion and Purpose is a blueprint of how an ordinary individual, fueled by an extraordinary purpose, can rally a community and raise life-changing funds for a cause they believe in. It chronicles my personal experiences, the triumphs, challenges, and lessons learned from saying "yes" to leading a fundraising campaign, to engaging others in a shared mission, to six-figure fundraising success which I never imagined we could achieve. Along the way, I discovered that the true power of fundraising lies in the heartfelt connections we build and the collective determination of a community united by purpose.

I write this book as a thank you and a challenge. It's a thank you to everyone who supported me, my family, my team, the thousands of fitness professionals and every donor who contributed. It's also a thank you to Mark, whose survival and friendship became the inspiration for everything that followed.

This book is dedicated to Mark Allen, who taught me the real meaning of heart and the importance of never giving up.

It is a challenge for you, the reader. I invite you to step forward and become a leader of impact in your own right. Whether your passion is heart health or another cause close to you, know that your willingness to act can spark miracles. You don't need to be a celebrity or a seasoned philanthropist to make a difference, I certainly wasn't. You need a passionate purpose and the courage to take the first step. The pages ahead will share how I took that step, and how you can too.

By the time you finish this book, I hope you feel empowered to launch your heartfelt fundraising journey. Together, we can create a ripple effect of positive change that carries forward for generations. Mark's story showed me that one prepared person can save a life; this journey showed me that one determined person can mobilize many, save countless lives, and transform an entire community.

Now, it's your turn to lead with heart.

– Devon G. Mitchell

Chapter 1: The Moment That Changed Everything

It was a great day for a triathlon. It's race day, all the training, the preparation, success was the focus, the quest to complete "50 races before 50," was in full focus.

I never imagined a single moment could alter the course of my life. The phone rang, and the voice on the other end of the line said Mark suffered a cardiac event at his triathlon Race. Silence, questions, tears, and all the emotions you could imagine showed up at the same time. I've never had this feeling in my adult life, so as my body was trying to process the words and handle the sudden overwhelming physical weakness, how do I process this information? I felt the tears running down my face, and then it hit me. The seconds felt like hours; the reality of the situation was that "my friend's life lies in the balance."

As I write this, I can feel a pit in my stomach and shakiness in my legs as if it was September 19, 2019.

He was rushed to the hospital, where doctors and nurses worked on him feverishly for over 40 minutes, fighting to get his heart beating again. It took a total of six shocks to stabilize Mark's heart rhythm. The medical team later said that his excellent physical fitness played a role in their decision to keep trying so long to revive him they believed his body could withstand the trauma and had a better chance of recovering. And they were right. Mark did make it, though it took some time. In the days that followed, he was unable to speak, eat, or walk. But with each passing week, he made strides that defied even his doctors' expectations. He had to relearn basic things and regain his strength through rehab, but his spirit and his faith were unbreakable. Within months, unbelievably, Mark was back at our gym not just to say hello, but to work out. Today, he exercises five days a week, back to work, he is living proof of purpose, faith, friendship and love.

That moment of crisis and the arduous recovery that followed changed me fundamentally. When I heard what happened to Mark, I felt utterly helpless knowing someone I care about hover between life and death. In that darkness, I also learned about the best of humanity: a stranger who didn't hesitate to help, paramedics and doctors who refused to give up, and a friend's sheer will to live. It underscored for me the importance of being prepared for emergencies and the vital role community support and knowledge play in saving lives. If even one link in that chain of survival had been missing the ending might have been very different. I cannot shake that thought. In a way, Mark's second chance became my second chance as well: an opportunity to reevaluate my purpose and priorities.

The critical importance of preparation and community health response. Mark's cardiac arrest taught me in the most visceral way that you can never underestimate the value of being prepared. Emergencies don't give you a warning or time to think; when they strike, action in the moment is everything. The volunteer who helped save my friend's life wasn't a doctor or a superhero in a cape. He was an ordinary person with extraordinary preparedness, someone who had taken the time to learn CPR and had the presence of mind to use it. That individual's readiness, combined with the rapid response of medical professionals, created a lifesaving bridge for Mark until advanced treatment could take over.

I began to see that heart health and emergency preparedness had to be a community effort. It wasn't just about our fitness or eating right, it was also about knowing what to do in a crisis and spreading that knowledge. The concept of community health response became very real to me. At our gym we invited our AHA local leaders to run bystander CPR training at the gym for members, because I kept thinking what if Mark's incident had happened in our gym or our neighborhood supermarket? Would people there know how to help? I wanted the answer to be yes.

Mark's story also gave me a new sense of responsibility as a community leader. I realized that, as a fitness coach and business owner, I was in a unique position to influence others positively. People look to us for guidance on how to live healthier lives; now I felt that guidance must include not just prevention of illness but also preparedness for emergencies. I started sharing Mark's story with anyone who would listen not to scare them, but to inspire them to take action: to learn CPR to know where the nearest defibrillators are when you are in a building, to support organizations like the American Heart Association that are fighting to improve emergency response and heart health for everyone.

Ultimately, this chapter of my life taught me that being ready to help is a crucial aspect of being truly healthy and part of a caring community. It's not enough for me to run a gym that helps people get fit; I want to be part of a community that looks out for each other's hearts, literally and figuratively. Preparation saves lives. Compassion moves people to act. When you combine the two, miracles happen.

Actionable Steps: How can you apply Mark's story to inform your preparation and advocacy? Here are a few steps to get started:

Learn CPR and First Aid. Take a course through your local Red Cross or an American Heart Association-certified class. Ensure you know how to perform hands-only CPR and use an AED. Encourage friends, family, and coworkers to get trained as well.

Identify your "Why." Think about why heart health or emergency preparedness matters to you. It could be a loved one's story, a personal health journey, or simply the desire to protect your community. Defining personal motivation will fuel your passion for any fundraising or advocacy work you undertake.

Connect Heart Health to Your Life or Business. Make a list of ways heart disease, stroke, or general wellness intersect with your daily life or profession. For example, do you work in a school, run a business, or lead a community group? Map out how improving heart health or emergency response knowledge could benefit those around you in those settings, discovering your opportunities to champion heart health in your immediate sphere of influence.

Chapter 2: Entering the Mission

In the wake of Mark's near-death experience and miraculous recovery, I found myself seeking ways to channel the gratitude and urgency I felt into something productive. The answer came soon after, in the form of an invitation to the Heart Ball the American Heart Association's annual gala in Philadelphia. I remember walking into that event with my wife, Samantha, feeling a mix of humility and excitement. The ballroom was decked out in red, uplighting and elegant decor, buzzing with hundreds of attendees in black-tie attire, all gathered for one purpose: to fight heart disease and celebrate survivors. It struck me that this was no ordinary charity event. The energy was a mix of celebratory and determined; you could sense that everyone in the room had been touched by heart disease or stroke in some way and was committed to making a difference.

As the program began, I listened intently to speakers ranging from top cardiologists to survivors sharing their testimonies. Each story, each statistic, and each expression of hope resonated deeply with me. When they announced Mark's name as an honoree and recounted his ordeal at the triathlon, tears welled up in my eyes. Seeing Mark alive, smiling, walking up to accept a recognition award was incredibly emotional. I glanced over at Samantha and saw she was wiping away tears as well. Our friend's survival was being celebrated as a triumph of community response and medical science, and here we were, witnessing it amid a crowd of people who truly understood its significance.

That night, I also started to realize how aligned my values and work were with the mission of the AHA. As owners of a health and wellness facility, Samantha and I have always tried to make our fitness environment more than just a place to exercise. From day one, we set out to create a community hub for wellness, a place where people feel supported in their health journeys. At the Heart Ball, I saw a mirror of that vision on a larger scale. The AHA was bringing the community together to support health and well-being, just as we aimed to do locally through fitness. The alignment with AHA's goals felt perfect. The commitment to preventing heart disease through promoting active, healthy lifestyles, research, education, and public health initiatives.

After the formal program, as the evening transitioned into dinner and mingling, I had conversations with AHA staff and volunteers. They spoke about the various programs the AHA supports, from funding cutting-edge cardiovascular research to community blood pressure screenings, to advocacy for healthier school lunches and CPR training in high schools. I was impressed by the breadth of the AHA's work. It was a glitzy gala night, and it was substantive, year-round efforts to save lives in every way imaginable. As a fitness professional, I was naturally drawn to their prevention and education initiatives. Still, I was also fascinated to learn about their focus on health equity working to ensure that resources and care reach underserved communities, because not everyone has equal access to health opportunities. It dawned (A-ha moment) on me that by partnering with AHA, I could expand the impact of what we were already doing in our gym and neighborhood. Together, we can tackle wellness from both grassroots and systemic levels.

Theme: Purpose-led partnerships and value-based leadership. When I reflect on why the Heart Ball had such a profound impact on me, it came down to this: I witnessed the power of purpose led partnerships in action. The event itself was a partnership between the AHA and community supporters (individuals and companies alike) who shared values around health and service. I realized that aligning with an organization whose mission resonates with your values can exponentially increase your impact. By joining forces, you create a sum greater than its parts.

The alignment was precise. The values of Fitness improving health, fostering community, empowering individuals align perfectly with the values of the AHA. This clarity of shared purpose became the foundation of my decision to say "yes" to deeper involvement. When your personal or business values align with a cause, your leadership in that space becomes authentic and powerful. People can sense when you are leading with genuine passion versus out of obligation. That authenticity attracts others to join you.

In my journey I recognized that I didn't have to fight heart disease or promote wellness alone. I could partner with a larger movement and lend my strengths to it. In doing so, I wasn't diluting my identity as an entrepreneur, a gym owner or as a leader, I was enhancing it. I used my platform and influence to benefit the community.

Saying yes to the Leaders of Impact opportunity was as much a business decision as it was a moral one. I knew that having Anytime Fitness associated with a cause like the

AHA would reinforce to our members and staff that we genuinely care about their well-being beyond membership fees or workouts. It demonstrated that we stand for something bigger – that our brand is about heart, literally and figuratively. This kind of purpose-driven leadership builds trust and loyalty. It also sets an example: by stepping up, my hoped was to encourage other local businesses and individuals to find causes they believe in and actively support them.

I learned that when you ground your leadership in purpose and values, and seek partnerships that reflect those, you create a collaborative environment for success. The cause benefits from your energy and resources; you benefit from the more profound meaning and community service brings into your life; and those around you benefit from the positive changes of your leadership. Everyone wins when values align, and collaborative partnerships are created.

Actionable Steps: When building purpose-led collaborative partnerships consider these steps:

Identify Organizations Aligned with Your Mission every meaningful partnership begins with alignment. Before signing an agreement or planning an event, step back and ask: *Who truly shares my mission?*

Start with research. Look into nonprofits, community organizations, schools, or advocacy groups that already stand for what you believe in. If your mission centers on health and wellness, explore heart health organizations, hospitals, or mental health initiatives. If your passion is education, consider programs focused on literacy, workforce training, or youth mentorship initiatives.

The key is to find natural intersections. Think of opportunities to discover partners that are willing to work side by side with you. The organizations that make you say, "*This is exactly what I care about*" are the ones that will unlock the most fruitful collaborations.

Craft and share your Community Wellness Story Partnerships are not only built on goals; they are built on trust. And trust is built on story. Your story, personal or organizational, is the heart of your brand. It conveys your values in a way that statistics and spreadsheets cannot. It explains why your mission matters, not just what it is.

For me, the story began with Mark's race day incident. It was a life-changing moment that forced us to see beyond physical fitness and into the more profound truth: health is life, and heart health must be a community priority. From that moment, our gym wasn't just about workouts, it was about saving lives. That story resonated because it was authentic. It was lived.

When you tell your story, you invite people to believe in your mission. For individuals, this could mean sharing a personal journey of recovery, resilience, or discovery. For organizations, it might be about showcasing the impact of a program or a pivotal moment of transformation.

Explore Collaborative Events
Partnerships thrive when they move from conversation to action. One of the most powerful ways to activate collaboration is through shared events.
Events create a stage for alignment to become visible.

They demonstrate shared values, leverage combined strengths, and open the door to new audiences. Consider:

- A charity fitness class that raises funds for a cause.
- A community wellness fair that brings multiple organizations together.

- A fundraising dinner or gala that highlights shared values.
- A speaking engagement or workshop that educates and empowers participants.

Sustain and Celebrate the Partnership
Collaborations are not "one-off" moments; they are seeds planted for long-term impact. After the event ends or the campaign concludes, take time to reflect with your team. What worked? What could be improved? And most importantly, celebrate. Share stories of success, highlight the lives that have been impacted, and honor your collaborators. Celebration strengthens the bond and inspires others to join.

After the Heart Ball, for example, I connected with the American Heart Association team about co-hosting heart-healthy workshops at our gym. That simple idea combined our audiences, reinforced our commitment to health, and deepened trust.

Chapter 3: Saying Yes with Purpose

The decision to officially join the Leaders of Impact campaign came from a nomination by my wife and the support of our two daughters, the only thing for me to do with that level of support was to say yes! However, it was not one I took lightly.

I remember the moment, what made me say "yes" was that my wife and our kids knew my heart and they wanted to share with American Heart Association's mission. What they did not know was that I had a feeling deep in my gut that this was what I was meant to do next.

I reflected on why we initially opened our fitness facility, and it was to build community, a chance to impact lives through health and fitness. Here was an opportunity to take that impact beyond the walls of our gym, beyond the day-to-day operations and into the community in a new way. It felt like a natural extension of what I was already doing.

Once I committed, I dove into planning with the same energy I'd bring to launching a new gym program or challenge. The campaign would run for seven weeks in the fall, and I set an ambitious goal for myself I wanted to raise $100,000 (a number that felt almost outlandish, considering I'd never raised funds like this before). The number was daunting, and it also motivated me. I thought that if this was going to help raise awareness for Mark's story and the AHA mission, then I had to dream big and make it count for the cause.

The next step was to map out what a great group of teammates would look like, qualities, expertise, energy, faith, purpose. I knew I couldn't do this alone. So, I started listing my top supporters and strategic partners the people who I believed would enthusiastically join this effort.

At the very top of the list was, of course, my wife Samantha and our two daughters. Samantha offered to handle a lot of the behind-the-scenes organizing, as she's incredibly skilled managing large programs and communication Our daughters helped with all the marketing, including social media and booths on the ground. I loved that they were proud and wanted to be involved.

Next on the list were my colleagues from the fitness industry. Our gym managers and trainers, as well as connections with over a dozen other fitness club owners and leaders in the region. We have a tight-knit network; many of us have gotten to know each other through conferences and online groups. If I rallied them, they could involve their gym communities, effectively multiplying our reach.

Then there were specific friends and mentors' people with wide networks or skills (such as photo and videography and event planning) whom I could tap for help. Lastly, I wrote down the businesses and community partners we'd worked with in the past (such as the local sporting goods store and the Chamber of commerce). These would be my "strategic partners" organizations that might sponsor events or donate after hearing our story.

Writing all those names and entities down and using the Look Within and Leverage (LWL) Model." It showed all the people and groups I could connect with to amplify the campaign. Seeing it drawn out was both empowering and humbling, empowering because I realized we had a larger network than I thought, and humbling because it showed how much support I would be relying on. It reminded me that leadership is not about going solo; it's about creating the environment and guiding your team toward a shared goal.

There was one more crucial element to saying yes with purpose: setting a community-wide goal that everyone could get behind, not just a dollar amount. After some thought, I framed my campaign to be about more than money. It was to raise awareness for CPR during the campaign and make healthy life choices. These were tangible impact goals that gave people something concrete to do, even if they couldn't donate much. It made the campaign more collaborative and inclusive for everyone to contribute to the mission.

So, there I was, with a mission statement in my heart, a rough plan on paper, and a growing team of supporters ready to mobilize. Hitting the "send" button on the email to the AHA, confirming my participation in Leaders of Impact, "excitement and nerves for the task ahead". I felt a surge of purpose flow through me. I wasn't just Devon the gym guy anymore, nor even just Devon the friend. I was Devon, the advocate and change agent, ready to lead beyond the walls of the Gym and into the broader community.

Theme: Expanding your identity as a change agent. One of the most profound personal shifts I experienced during this process was embracing an expanded identity. We all carry titles or roles that define us by profession, relationships, community standing. I was an entrepreneur, a coach, a husband, a father, and a friend. Now I was an advocate, a philanthropist and an American Heart Association Leader of Impact participant. At first, it felt almost presumptuous to claim those titles.

Who was I to lead a major fundraising campaign? I wasn't a celebrity or a wealthy philanthropist. I was just a regular guy who wanted to help share the how CPR and the work of The American Heart Association saved my friend's life. But that's precisely where the power of this experience revealed itself: The willingness to embrace growth while leveraging leadership for a cause that creates an impact.

Saying "yes" with purpose meant I allowed myself to step outside my comfort zone. It's like pushing through a task when you don't feel like it. I found I had more to give, more to become, when I aligned with a higher purpose. I want to emphasize that anyone can use the Look Within and Leverage Model (LWL). You don't need permission or a specific job title to participate. By deciding to champion a cause you become an ambassador for that cause and it empowers everything about you. I started noticing that in everyday conversations whether I was at the gym, the supermarket, social event I was now naturally bringing up why I support the American Heart Association and the leader of impact campaign. It wasn't forced; it was just part of who I was becoming. My passion was integrating into my identity.

This expansion of identity was also contagious. As I fully embraced being a leader of impact, people around me responded. Some began to see themselves as part of something larger as well, they became fundraisers and heart health ambassadors among their families and friends. By stepping up, I had implicitly permitted others to do the same. That's a critical lesson in leadership: when you lead by example with clarity of purpose, you invite others to join you and tap into their leadership potential.

In summary, this chapter taught me that saying yes to a cause-driven opportunity can redefine who you are in the best way possible. It pushes you to grow into new roles and discover strengths you didn't know you had. It also shows everyone watching that they, too, can make a difference. My identity was now intertwined with this mission, and it felt incredibly fulfilling. I was leading with purpose, and that sense of purpose became the driving force behind every effort we made during the campaign.

Actionable Steps: Are you ready to say "yes" to your cause or campaign? Here's how to infuse it with purpose and set the stage for success:

Write Your Mission Statement. Clearly articulate why you are taking on the cause, campaign or project. One or two sentences that capture your motivation and goals. Post this mission statement somewhere visible. It will serve as your north star and keep you focused when things get busy.

Set Specific Goals (Personal and community). Determine a fundraising target and consider impact goals (such as the number of people educated, events held, or policies changed). Having both personal goals (what you want to achieve) and community goals (what you want others to gain) will give your campaign depth and meaning. For example, aim to raise a certain amount and to involve a certain number of people in the effort.

Identify Your Top 10 Supporters/Partners. Create a list of the first ten people or organizations you will contact once you start. These should be folks likely to say "yes" and offer significant help or donations. Think of close friends, family members, business partners, or mentors who believe in you. Contact them early, share your mission, and invite them to take on a role or pledge support. Getting key allies on board early creates momentum and confidence.

Chapter 4: Defining Leaders of Impact

Core Story: When I officially entered the Leaders of Impact campaign the AHA held a campaign orientation meeting (held virtually over Zoom, since our group spanned multiple cities), I met the other nominees and participants. We were approximately 295 individuals across the country that year, in different cities and regions, all ready to make a difference. I remember looking at the gallery of faces on the screen a mosaic of leaders, business owners, healthcare professionals, community volunteers. Some had personal stories like mine; others had a passion for the cause. Despite our different backgrounds, there was this shared sense of purpose in everyone's eyes, and an eagerness to lead and serve.

The AHA campaign coordinators explained process and purpose of competition, "Over a 7-week competition, you and your Impact Team will educate your community about heart disease, advocate for health, and raise essential funds for lifesaving research. At the end of the campaign, one standout nominee will be celebrated as the local Leaders of Impact winner, and the top nominee nationwide will be named the National Leaders of Impact

Winner". The phrase "Leaders of Impact" began to hold profound meaning for me. For me success would not just be measured by how much lifesaving funds I would raise, it would also be measured buy by how many people we could impact and share the mission of the American Heart Association.

I knew that it would take a collaborative effort, so I started thinking of all the people I had put on my team. This would be an ideal opportunity to use the Look Within and Leverage (LWL) Model to identify potential donors and helpers to with a sense of ownership within the campaign. If I inspire a dozen other people to step up and lead mini efforts within our campaign, then our reach would grow exponentially.

One concrete step I took was creating an official campaign team. Captains led different efforts to grow impact and drive awareness. For example, our eldest daughter brought her influencer status and social media expertise to lead our digital presence. A friend volunteered to support the fundraising event. Samantha coordinated and led our calendar of fundraising events; this collaborative effort was the (LWL Model at work.) It signaled that this wasn't my campaign, it was our collective campaign.

We also set up regular team calls to share progress and ideas. In these meetings, we celebrated every success and highlighted contributions, no matter how small. We all recognized our contributions as a collective achievement.

One of my favorite collaborative tools we created was a shared campaign calendar. We used a simple online calendar to mark all our planned activities, including CPR training dates, fundraiser events, social media content days and deadlines. Everyone on the team had access to it. This way not only were we organized, but each person could see how their piece fit into the bigger picture and could rally others around upcoming activities.

As the campaign progressed, I noticed something beautiful: friends were introducing their friends into the effort, colleagues were reaching out to their networks, and our circle of impact was widening. For instance, one colleague created a list of team member employer to match all donations from their employees to our campaign. These were initiatives I didn't micromanage or even initially imagine emerged naturally because everyone was empowered to contribute and lead form their position of expertise and experience once they joined.

Through this, I developed a deep appreciation for clearing the runway and creating the environment for success. Being in action providing direction and resources and supporting them as they made things happen. This ripple effect of individual efforts creates a ripple effect of leadership and is what truly drives change.

Theme: Collaboration, not competition is a competitive edge. Traditional thinking sometimes portrays leadership as a solo act for one person at the front, taking charge, and getting credit. But the Leaders of Impact experience shattered that notion for me. Real impact comes when you are empowered and mission focused. It's about collaboration.

Yes, I was aware that it was a competition and I was competing to be the National Leader of Impact Winner by the end of the 7-week campaign. Ultimately, we were on the same team fundraising for lifesaving research.

Emphasize collaboration as a team pillar; all contributions have value. If you have an excellent idea for a mini fundraising event, run with it and let them shine as the lead. If a family member wants to take charge of a particular task, step back and let them own it and you provide support; everyone had a vested interest in the outcome. We work harder and more joyfully on something they feel is theirs, not just a favor for someone else.

Collaboration also meant being open to partnering with other organizations and groups. We weren't afraid to ask for help or to join forces. For example, we teamed up with AHA for a hands-on CPR demonstration and awareness at our facility. They brought equipment and instructors, we brought participants, and together we raised awareness for dozens of people in life-saving skills. It wasn't officially part of our fundraising drive, but it helped forward the mission.

Yes, some of those individuals later donated or supported our campaign. That's the power of alignment: two groups working together can achieve more than each group could on its own.

I view competition in this context "as solution vs. the problem." The real competition was against heart disease and against the lack of visibility that enables healthy outcomes. Every collaborative effort was a win against that opponent. Every new person who learned more about CPR, every additional donor, and every partnership scored points for the cause.

By redefining leadership as a shared endeavor, I discovered that people were eager to assume new responsibilities. Many told me later that being part of this campaign awakened their sense of purpose or leadership that they hadn't previously tapped into. That is as great a victory as any dollar amount raised. We were building a community of changemakers.

Actionable Steps: To foster collaborative leadership and a team-driven campaign, try these actions:

Make a "Look Within and Leverage Map." (LWL MAP) Draw a diagram or list of all the groups and individuals you could involve friends, family, colleagues, social groups, local businesses, etc. Consider how each could be connected to your journey and how their unique stories and skillsets can be incorporated (in terms of skills, resources, and outreach). This visual will help you plan your collaboration and ensure you don't leave any potential partners untapped.

Team Captains or Co-Leads. Identify a few reliable supporters and give each leadership role for a segment of your campaign (social media, Event Coordinator, Community Outreach, etc.). Empower them with autonomy and a small team. When people have clear ownership, they feel a sense of pride and responsibility, which in turn boosts overall progress.

Use Shared Planning Tools. Create a shared calendar or project board that is accessible to your team, where all events, deadlines, and tasks are visible. Regularly update it and encourage team members to add their activities. Keep everyone in sync and foster a sense of shared mission. Consider holding weekly or biweekly check-in meetings (known as "LWL Huddles,") depending on the length of your fundraising campaign, celebrating wins, troubleshooting issues, and maintaining momentum.

Chapter 5: The Power of Community

Core Story: Midway through the campaign, I experienced a moment so powerful that it still brings a lump to my throat when I recall it. It happened at the Anytime Fitness Annual Conference. This conference was a gathering of thousands of fitness professionals franchise owners, managers, trainers from all over the world my extended Anytime Fitness family.

Mark was being honored as one of the Anytime Fitness member success winners. I knew the final product would be awesome and a great opportunity to highlight Mark's remarkable journey, but I had no idea just how until the video was shown to all in attendance.

In that vast conference hall over 2,000 fitness professionals strong, the video recounted the triathlon incident, the CPR rescue, the hospital, the rehab and Mark's resilient spirit to recovery. As the video played, I could sense the stillness in the room, everyone hanging onto the voice of the narrator and the gravity of the story. It's hard to describe the emotion in that room. Tears and cheers all together. Fitness professionals from different states and countries empathized with and embraced Mark's story because they, too, have members who are resilient and have persevered through challenges. Each other, inspired by what we were collectively part of Owners, trainers, staff everyone in attendance. "This is for Mark; this is for all of us." It was as if every individual effort merged into one giant wave of support. I had never felt anything like it.

I stayed in my seat for a bit before joining Mark, his wife and Samantha, on stage as he accepted the Member success award! After accepting the award Mark asked me to share with the audience, little did I know that this would have a profound impact on my leadership and my relationship with Anytime Fitness.

At that moment I couldn't control my tears anymore, they were flowing and I couldn't nor did I want them to stop because the realization that I saved my friend's life was real and present. I am in tears now! folks expressing their support, offering to host events at their gyms, wanting to collaborate on awareness campaigns, and simply sharing how moved they were. It became clear that Mark's story and our mission had transcended our local community and touched a national network of fitness professionals. It reinforced a beautiful truth: when a community rallies around a shared purpose, its power is limitless. The energy in that conference hall the collective heart of 2,000 plus people beating as one – propelled our campaign to heights I hadn't dared to imagine. It also forged bonds among us; we all felt like we were on the same team that day, part of something far bigger than any single gym or person.

Theme: Collective energy and shared purpose elevate everything. The conference experience was a living example of the adage "the whole is greater than the sum of its parts." I witnessed how shared purpose can electrify a crowd and push the limits of what's possible. Individually, we all cared about health and Fitness, however collectively there was a purposeful focus on supporting Mark's next chapter in his journey.

The key lesson for any fundraising or community effort is to create a rallying moment. We often look for a reason to come together, a cause that allows us to feel part of something meaningful alongside others. When you provide that focal point whether it's an event, a story, a goal, you activate the goodwill and enthusiasm in your community. In our case, the focal point was Mark's journey, which became my journey, and ultimately, our community's journey. Something that symbolizes unity, such as a group walk, a collective online campaign, or a shared challenge. The important thing is that it's done together.

I also learned that emotion and authenticity fuel collective energy. The reason the conference moment caught fire is that it was deeply genuine. It wasn't scripted that way; it came from raw human connection. People were moved by the real story of a life saved and a friend trying to make a difference. Authenticity is powerful. It reminds you that while strategies and plans are essential, at the heart of every successful campaign lies genuine emotion and human connection. Embrace your passion and purpose and people will see and feel hope, empathy, urgency, and joy because those feelings inspire action more than any fact or figure. The collective energy of a rallying cry or symbol that builds momentum.

One person can light a spark; it takes a community to build a roaring fire. And when that fire is built, it warms and illuminates everyone it touches. The communal success of that day became a cornerstone of our campaign's identity, giving us the confidence and drive to push even harder toward our goals.

Actionable Steps: To harness the power of the community in your efforts, consider the following steps:

Plan a Unifying Moment. Create at least one event or campaign moment where you, your team and the community can participate simultaneously. It could be a live gathering (such as a kickoff event, a special presentation, or a group run) or a virtual one (a coordinated social media blast, live stream, or "Day of Giving"). Build anticipation for it and make it a celebratory and meaningful experience. A shared experience galvanizes your community.

Create a Rallying Cry or Symbol. Develop a simple slogan, hashtag, or even a song or playlist that embodies the spirit of your campaign. Use it consistently. For example, a short motto on everyone's shirts or a hashtag used when posting about your cause helps foster unity. It gives people something to share and feel part of.

Encourage Storytelling and Testimonials. Invite members of your community to share their reasons for supporting the cause or their personal experiences with it. At events or on social media to feature your story. When people hear each other's "why," it deepens the collective resolve; it could be open mic moments at an event or spotlight posts online (e.g., "Supporter of the Week" story). This recognizes individuals and a shared purpose across your community.

Chapter 6: What Surprised Me Most

I initially thought I knew what the American Heart Association did things like funding research on heart disease and promoting exercise. However, once I became deeply involved in the campaign, I was amazed by the breadth and depth of the AHA's work. The biggest surprise wasn't a single moment, but rather a series of eye-opening realizations that unfolded throughout my journey.

Early in the campaign, the AHA provided us, Leaders of Impact, with educational materials to help us discuss the cause. Through this, I discovered facets of the AHA's mission I hadn't been aware of. For example, I learned that the AHA is heavily invested in public education, not just advising people to eat healthily, but also teaching practical, life-saving skills like CPR in schools and workplaces. They have programs that support and empower kids, such as initiatives to ensure healthier school lunches and encourage physical activity among youth. As a parent, it stuck with me that prevention starts early, and habits formed in childhood can last a lifetime.

Another surprise was the AHA's strong focus on advocacy and policy change. They weren't only funding scientists in labs (though they do plenty of that, as one of the largest funders of cardiovascular research in the world); they were also in the halls of Congress and state legislatures, championing laws for a healthier nation. I came across stories of the AHA helping pass laws to require newborn heart defect screenings, pushing for tobacco control laws, and improving systems of care for stroke victims. I realized heart health isn't just an individual pursuit; it's something that the environment and policies around us can significantly shape. The AHA was tackling heart disease from every angle from the personal level, CPR training and community health programs to policies and access to care Advocacy.

What truly inspired me was seeing the ripple effect of these efforts on the lives of real people, including those around me. For instance, after I shared some AHA nutrition resources, folks added blood pressure checks, adjusted eating habits, increased activity levels and made other lifestyle changes. Small changes spurred action to improve lives and create victories.

I was surprised by the scope of impact we were able to have in such a short time. In just those seven weeks of campaigning, beyond raising money, we saw some lives directly touched like donors who later shared stories of their visits and encouraged others to see a cardiologist because of something they learned from our campaign. I realized that the AHA's work creates a domino effect: one piece of information or one program can lead to a chain of events that ultimately save or improve lives, even if it's not immediately apparent.

Awareness and education are as powerful as research in combating cardiovascular disease. It's the knowledge shared and acted upon in communities that creates a ripple effect of wellness. Conducting a hands-on CPR class might equip someone to save a life, like the healthcare volunteer who saved Mark. A pamphlet on recognizing a stroke could prompt someone to call 911 sooner and prevent long-term disability. A healthy cooking workshop could lead to a family changing their diet and potentially reducing their risk of heart disease in the future.

We often think of prominent organizations in terms of large-scale projects, such as million-dollar research grants. Those are critical, but what's just as powerful are the small-scale interventions that make a difference and adds up across the country and the globe, the support groups for heart patients, the blood pressure screening drives, the pamphlets in community centers. These are relatively simple things that have an immense cumulative impact. And the AHA was orchestrating all of it, often behind the scenes, empowering local volunteers to carry the torch.

This realization has a key takeaway for any fundraiser or advocate: understand the full scope of your cause and communicate it effectively. People might assume they know what a charitable organization does, but when they learn the whole story, they often become more passionate supporters. When I told donors, "Your contribution isn't just funding lab research; it's also training a teenager to do CPR, and educating a family about healthy eating, and helping fight for better health laws," their eyes lit up. It connected the dots between their donation and real-world outcomes they could visualize.

I also saw how wellness advocacy (like what I was doing at the gym) ties into healthcare. Workouts and nutrition advice we give at the gym aren't separate from the fight against heart disease they are front-line defenses in that fight. Every mile run, every healthy meal choice is a small victory in preventing heart issues.

The ecosystem of change that a cause like the American Heart Association creates. It reinforced why fundraising mattered how funding a single project fueling an entire movement of health improvement, from the laboratory to the living room. And each one of us, by spreading awareness and leading with purpose and passion could amplify that movement in your circles of influence, causing ripples that extend far beyond our immediate reality.

Actionable Steps: To broaden awareness and create your ripple effect in advocacy, try these actions:

Host an Expert Talk or Workshop. Invite a local doctor, nutritionist, or AHA representative to speak to your group (friends, workplace, gym, etc.) about heart health and prevention. A short talk or Q&A session can enlighten and motivate people. Making it a community event (virtual or in-person) helps spread knowledge further, as attendees often share what they learn with their families.

Share Educational Content Regularly. Become an information hub for your network, sharing a "Heart-Healthy Tip of the Week" on your social media or bulletin board. Use reputable sources, such as the AHA's website or literature. Over time, these small bits of information accumulate and can change attitudes and behaviors. Consistency is key regularly sharing keeps heart health in people's minds year-round.

Connect Fitness to Advocacy. If you're involved in Fitness or any wellness activity, explicitly tie it to heart health in your messaging. For example, organize a group walk or run where participants also learn about heart-healthy habits. Encourage participants to discuss their reasons for participating. These frames exercise not just as personal fitness, but as part of a larger cause healthier communities, which can inspire others to join or start their healthy journeys.

Chapter 7: Our Campaign Story

The success of my Leaders of Impact campaign was, at its heart, a family and team victory. From day one, I knew I had an incredible advantage: my immediate family and my work family were completely behind me, ready to roll up their sleeves and support me.

At home, my wife, Samantha, and our daughters became my brainstorming team of advisors and emotional support crew. Many evenings, our dining table became a campaign headquarters. Over dinner, we would toss around ideas for fundraisers, social media posts hashtags and overall support. Our girls came up with the idea of hosting a "Healthy Heart" fashion and dance mini-fundraiser and awareness event.

They led the effort engaged their network to make it happen. It was a fantastic event on heart health that helped with campaign fundraising. That was purely our daughters' initiative, and it brought a different perspective and demographic to the campaign.

Samantha, meanwhile, was the unsung hero throughout this journey. Natanya handled a significant portion of the logistics, including scheduling meetings, coordinating with the AHA staff, tracking donations, and sending thank-you notes, all while ensuring our events ran smoothly. Naomi led the effort to ensure participants' documents were checked in at the event.

Their leadership in organizing was on full display and was indispensable. Samantha had it all mapped out: she had volunteers assigned, supplies purchased, timings set, and even contingency plans in place. The event went off without a hitch, largely thanks to her meticulous planning.

The campaign also drew in our extended family, who became long-distance cheerleaders, calling relatives and their friends to share with them what we were doing, effectively fundraising and spreading awareness on our behalf.

All these threads family, friends, colleagues, and company worked together to support and deliver our campaign's story. It wasn't about one person's actions; it was about how each of us contributed our unique talents and connections, (The Look Within and Leverage Model "LWL") and every engagement was a testament to collaboration and love. In that moment, I felt an overwhelming sense of gratitude. The real victory was not just the money raised, but the community that had rallied and strengthened around this cause.

Family-led change + team execution = campaign success. Our story illustrates how combining the personal touch of family with the organizational power of a team drives a campaign to success. Family brings heart and unity when your family is involved, the mission permeates your daily life and there's a deep, shared commitment. A supportive family will fuel you on the tough days and celebrate with you on the good ones. They also often have their networks (schools, workplaces, social circles) that can be engaged, effectively extending your reach.

On the other hand, the involvement of a professional team or community group brings structure and breadth. My staff and colleagues provided skills and bandwidth that I didn't have on my own. They helped execute ideas and introduced new ones.

When done correctly, a team functions like a well-oiled machine: each part does what it does best, all moving toward a common goal. What I experienced was that the intersection of family passion and team professionalism was where the magic happened. The enthusiasm from my family motivated the team, and the team's success feedback loop further invigorated my family. Leadership can be distributed without losing personal touch. I did not have or needed to know every detail personally for things to go well. In fact, by trusting my team, they were empowered to take the campaign as their own. My role often became one of coordinator and facilitator ensuring everyone had what they needed and felt appreciated. That not only prevented burnout for everyone, but it also allowed others to lead with ownership.

Our mission was also evident in how we combined our personal and business identities. The campaign wasn't something separate from our day-to-day lives; it became an integral part of our family routine and business operations. There was no rigid boundary, such as "work on campaign during a set time only flowed naturally through our lives, making it enjoyable. This blending of worlds created a strong, unified front we were all one team, regardless of our role.

The campaign's success was a direct result of the collaborative spirit. It's incredible what people can accomplish when they join forces across family and professional lines. Everyone brings something valuable to the table. And when you acknowledge that and let them contribute, the outcome is multiplied. The whole becomes something so much more dynamic and resilient than what any one of us could have built alone.

Actionable Steps: To create purposeful alignment through family involvement and team execution in your campaign, consider these steps:

Assign Core Team Roles (Including Family). Meet with your closest supporters whether they are relatives or colleagues and divvy up key roles. Who will handle finance tracking and donations? Who will lead event planning? Who manages communications (emails, social media)? Clarify these roles early. Don't shy away from assigning official duties to family members, they are team members. Kids can have roles too (e.g., creating art, spreading the word at school, helping pack event materials). Clear roles prevent confusion and ensure all aspects of the campaign are covered.

Working together to develop a family- and team-inspired campaign theme could involve creating a slogan, logo, or hashtag that everyone uses. For example, if your last name is Quamina, perhaps "Team Quamina Heart Heroes" becomes a reality, and you create a little heart hero logo that you use on flyers and T-shirts. Involving everyone in this creative process makes it fun and invests them emotionally. Additionally, a consistent theme or branding makes your campaign recognizable and memorable to the public.

Hold regular family or team meetings or Check-Ins this establishes a routine check-in for your campaign crew. It could be a Sunday night family huddle to plan the week, or a quick mid-week Zoom with key team members. Keep these meetings positive and solution oriented. Use them to review progress, assign new tasks, and crucially, to acknowledge effort. For example, each meeting starts by thanking someone for a specific contribution that week ("Thank you to Natanya for designing that awesome flyer!"). These sync-ups keep everyone aligned, motivated, and feeling appreciated.

Testimonial - Samantha Mitchell (Wife & Campaign Logistics Lead): "Working on this campaign with Devon has been a life-changing experience for our family. We poured our hearts into it together from our daughters organizing the fashion and dance fundraiser to the countless nights planning events. I watched Devon Inspire not just our gym, but also the community. Seeing our girls learn the value of giving back, I realized this campaign wasn't just about fundraising; it was about family and community coming alive with a sense of purpose. It's something I'll forever be proud of."

Chapter 8: What I'm Most Proud Of

When I look back on the entire journey, from the moment I learned about Mark's incident to the culmination of the campaign, many accomplishments could fill me with pride. We raised a Six-Figure sum to support the lifesaving work of American Heart Association. We raise awareness for heart health, CPR and potentially saved lives indirectly through our efforts. But the things I find myself most proud of aren't numbers or statistics. It's the people, the way our Anytime Fitness community and extended network rose to the occasion and supported our Campaign.

It struck me that our campaign had become self-sustaining at that moment. It was no longer about me trying to motivate people; everyone was encouraged to do so. They understood the mission and were pushing it forward on their initiative. I felt like a proud parent watching a child learn to walk and then run on their own. The community we built was running with the cause, and that told me that what we created would last beyond the campaign itself.

Community members signed up for gym membership, lifestyles changes, increased physical activity and the sense of community as the reason. It was like planting seeds and seeing a garden bloom. It's like seeing someone learn how to ride a bicycle (from wobbles to full blown rider).

When asked what I'm most proud of, I think of moments of empowerment. Our campaign became a catalyst for personal growth and community empowerment. We didn't just raise funds; we raised a stronger community. We ignited a spirit of collaboration and humility that will continue to burn long after the official campaign has ended. And knowing that people feel ownership of that spirit that they feel they made it happen (which they did!) is the greatest reward of all.

Theme: Empowering others creates exponential results. The journey taught me that true success in a campaign isn't measured only by the immediate outcomes, but by how it transforms the people involved. When you empower others, you're not just adding to the effort; you're multiplying it. Each person who grows into a leader or advocate can inspire many more, and thus the impact has greater growth.

I realized that empowerment often starts with trust and encouragement. By entrusting roles to my team and volunteers, by encouraging them to try new things, it signaled a belief in them. In return, they often exceeded their expectations. A campaign can be a fantastic platform for people to discover their talents and passion for service. It gives a shared mission that folks can latch onto as they step outside their comfort zones.

Another aspect of empowerment is recognition and gratitude. When your teammates feel appreciated, it fuels their desire to do even more. Our campaign celebrated every win and every person who contributed to it.

One of the practical strategies we used was documenting milestones and sharing them. For example, each time we reached a fundraising milestone, we would debrief our efforts to identify specific actions that contributed to our success. By highlighting these, we leveraged the team's efforts and gained evidence of our impact. It was our achievement.

The exponential magic happened when everyone involved felt a sense of ownership and pride. By empowering those around me, we didn't just accomplish a one-time campaign; we built capacity in people. We helped individuals realize their potential to make a difference. That's a legacy. The AHA will spend the funds raised on great programs, but the confidence, compassion, and leadership skills developed in our community remain and will fuel future great works. For any reader of this book, remember lifting others is the surest way to rise higher yourself and to ensure your impact doesn't end with you alone.

Actionable Steps: To maximize impact by empowering others and celebrating shared success, try these steps:

Celebrate Small Wins Publicly. Don't wait until the end to acknowledge success. Create a culture of celebration throughout your campaign. For instance, send out weekly updates highlighting something positive "This week's shout-out goes to our volunteer crew who packed 100 healthy snack kits!" or "We've reached 25% of our goal thank you to everyone, especially Naomi, who brought in 10 new donors!". Public recognition (be it in meetings, emails, or social media) makes people feel valued and seen.

Keep a Journal or Scrapbook. Document the journey in real-time. Create a scrapbook with photos and notes or a shared digital album. Encourage team members to contribute, maybe someone writes a paragraph about an event, or another shares a few photos. Create a keepsake and a living testament during the campaign that people can look at and say, "Wow, look at all we've done!" It reinforces the collective achievement and can be deeply motivating. After the campaign, it becomes a treasured record of what you all accomplished together.

Thank Every Contributor Personally. Make it a non-negotiable task to thank every single person who helped or donated, regardless of the amount or role they played: personalized handwritten thank-you notes, a personalized email, or a quick phone call. Mention specifically what you appreciate (e.g., "Thank you for volunteering at the Fun Run, your energy kept everyone motivated!" or "Your $5 donation mattered it helped fund the important work."). People are more likely to stay engaged or support again in the future when they feel their contribution was noticed and appreciated. Plus, it's the right thing to do to honor the generosity and effort people have put in.

Chapter 9: Leading into the Future

The campaign concluded on a high note. At the end of our seven-week fundraising and outreach blitz, we not only met our goals we surpassed them. I was notified that I had been honored as the National Leader of Impact Winner for 2023. It was a humbling and exhilarating moment to be recognized by the American Heart Association. My full circle moment was attending the Philadelphia Heart Ball (the same heart ball event I attended only a year ago, now I was standing on a stage sharing the journey and accepting an award in front of a crowd of AHA supporters and fellow changemakers from across the region. As I held the award, I reflected on everything that brought me there. It wasn't just the seven-week campaign; it was the culmination of a journey that started with one life-altering incident at a triathlon and evolved into a mission that I know will last a lifetime.

On that stage, I shared Mark's story and our community's efforts. The AHA was celebrating its centennial a hundred years of impact and entering its second century of work and to be a part of that history was both humbling and inspiring. There was a palpable sense that, while we should be proud of our progress, there is still much to do, the future of making heart health equitable for all.

After the formalities, I had the opportunity to mingle with AHA executives, scientists, and other volunteers. A conversation that left a deep imprint on me was with an AHA researcher who thanked me for what our campaign raised, explaining how those funds might support projects in the coming year like hypertension control initiative in underserved communities. It made me realize that our six-figure success was not an endpoint, but a fuel injection for ongoing efforts.

That money would translate into blood pressure cuffs, educational programs, maybe even policy advocacy to improve food access in those communities. In other words, the finish line of our campaign was the starting line for real-world impact enabled by those funds.

My hope for the future. For the American Heart Association as it embarks on its next hundred years, I envision an era of unprecedented innovation and inclusivity.

My hope is American Heart Association will continue to break new ground in science, discovering cures and highly effective treatments for conditions such as heart failure and stroke. But equally important, I hope the organization continues to break down barriers so that these advances reach everyone.

A phrase that often comes up in AHA discussions is "health equity", and I saw firsthand what that means. It means focusing on social determinants of health things like the safety of your neighborhood for exercise, the availability of healthy food, the quality of local healthcare, all of which can contribute to disparities in heart health outcomes. For instance, during the campaign, I learned that life expectancy can vary by up to 20 years in neighborhoods just a few miles apart, due to such inequities that's staggering and unacceptable. My sincere hope is that in the future, organizations like AHA, together with community partners, can close those gaps.

In that vision of the future, I see Anytime Fitness and other wellness brands playing a key role. After all, we are on the front lines of community health every day. The possibility of developing programs that gyms across the country can adopt.

On a more personal level, I wanted to continue being a Leader of Impact beyond the award title. Winning national recognition is terrific, but what truly matters is what you do with that platform. For me, that means mentoring future Leaders of Impact participants, sharing tips and lessons from my experience. I want to see others surpass what we did keep raising the fundraising bar, come up with new creative outreach ideas, and engage even more people. Progress is a relay race; I've run my leg and now I'm eager to pass the baton.

At the heart of my hope for the future is the belief that the American Heart Association continues the mission with passion, advocacy, and collaboration extending to more individuals, communities, businesses.

We've seen how deadly heart disease can be, but also how preventable and beatable it is with the proper knowledge, care, engagement and support. The future I see is one where heart disease is far less common because we've invested in preventative tools and build sustainable systems every workplace and school has an AED and people trained to use it; where no one is afraid to call for help because they can't afford it or because of language barriers and where staying heart-healthy is woven into the fabric of daily life for everyone.

Standing at that awards gala, I realized that although one chapter our campaign was coming to an end, a new one was beginning. I felt an immense sense of responsibility not to let the flame we ignited die out. Leading into the future means keeping that flame burning and lighting others with it. And I couldn't be more excited to continue that work, with all the lessons and love that got us this far.

Theme: Long-term wellness, equity, and sustained community partnerships. The future of heart health advocacy, as I see it, rests on two pillars: innovation and inclusion. Innovation will bring us better treatments, more innovative ways to educate and engage people, and new strategies to encourage healthy lifestyles. Inclusion will ensure those innovations reach every heart in every community. It's not enough to advance; we must advance together, leaving no heart behind.

For sustained impact, partnerships must continue to grow and evolve. The campaign taught me the value of cross-sector partnership when businesses, nonprofits, schools, and local governments work hand in hand, the reach is magnified. I hope to see more gyms partnering with AHA, more restaurants offering heart-healthy options, more tech companies creating apps and devices that support cardiac wellness, and more policies that make healthy choices easier and unhealthy choices harder. (like access to locally grown food, urban planning for active living, etc.)

Equitable heart health also means tailoring approaches to community needs. What works in one neighborhood might not support the needs of another. The next century involves a great deal of listening and collaboration at the grassroots level, empowering local leaders to address unique challenges. In a way, the Leaders of Impact campaign itself is an example of this: it gives local changemakers the tools and platforms to improve their communities in transformative ways.

I envision fitness facilities as wellness hubs were lifting weights, running on treadmills, Yoga, functional training and movement, nutrition coaching, including new and cutting-edge technologies true centers of health promotion. where health screenings can happen, where support groups meet, where information is disseminated. Fitness facilities become wellness center and can be the connective tissue between people and resources. leveraging the story of our campaign to show what's possible.

Ultimately, I hope that in the future we'll have more stable funding for health prevention and a culture so well-informed and proactive that heart disease rates will plummet. That's a far-off vision, maybe not so far off, but every step towards that vision counts.

As we lead into the future, the lesson I carry is that together we are unstoppable. The momentum we built is transformative and it continues to grow. In our case, we turned a personal crisis into a community triumph. Imagine turning community triumphs into national movements, and national movements into global change. One heart at a time, one community at a time, that's how we build a heart-healthy world for future generations.

Actionable Steps: To contribute to the future of equitable heart health and sustained impact, consider these forward-looking actions:

Create a Community Health Pledge. Draft a pledge or charter with your community (could be your workplace, gym, school, or neighborhood) that commits to heart-healthy and inclusive practices. For example, consider pledging to host annual CPR training sessions, advocating for healthy food options in your local community, connecting with hospitals and clinics and leveraging their resources of local health professionals such as cardiologists, researchers or ensuring that your events are accessible to people of all backgrounds. Having a written pledge that members sign onto can solidify a long-term commitment and act as a reminder to uphold those values.

Establish Ongoing Partnerships. Identify at least one local partnership that can carry on beyond a single campaign. It could involve adopting a school to provide wellness workshops annually, teaming up with a local clinic for free screening days, or partnering with a community center for an annual Heart Health awareness campaign. Create an agreement or plan that makes the collaboration recurring consistency builds trust and has a more profound impact over time.

Inspire Others with Your Story. Don't let your journey live in a vacuum share it to spark more change. Submit your story to your local news outlet, the American Heart Association or other relevant organizations. Share the lessons learned and encourage the next wave of leaders. Consider also mentoring a new volunteer or campaigner being a guide for someone else multiplies the impact of your experience.

Epilogue:

As I close this book and reflect on the incredible journey we've taken together through these pages, one message shines through above all: purpose-driven fundraising is the future of philanthropy and community building. In a world where people crave connection and authenticity, aligning your heartfelt passion with tangible action is the key to unlocking both generosity and impact on a scale you might never have imagined.

I titled this book Heartfelt Fundraising: Mastering Six-Figure Success with Passion and Purpose, but the truth is, the dollar figure impressive as six digits may be is just one measure of success.

The real "mastery" achieved is the understanding that success is best when it is shared among a team, a community, or the beneficiaries. It's the success of knowing that every person who contributed or participated feels a part of that success and can take pride in it. It's the success of seeing a ripple effect: one act of leadership inspiring another, one healed heart leading to many more protected hearts. I hope the stories and steps in these chapters have not only informed you but also inspired you to believe that you, too, can step up and lead a heartfelt fundraising journey of your own. Because you absolutely can. You've seen how an ordinary person like me, with no celebrity name, no extraordinary wealth, and juggling the responsibilities of business and family, managed to rally a community and make a significant impact. If I could do it, so can you.

Perhaps your cause is heart health, like mine, or maybe it's something else entirely, such as cancer research, environmental conservation, youth mentorship, mental health awareness or animal rescue. The causes worthy of passion are numerous. Whatever it is that tugs at your heartstrings, whatever problem in the world that keeps you up at night, or a story that brings tears to your eyes that might be your calling. Don't ignore that tug. Follow it, embrace it.

Each of us can lead, and leadership begins with caring enough to act and inviting others to join. You don't need to have all the answers or a detailed roadmap from the start. You need to begin. Perhaps that means reaching out to an organization and saying, "I want to help." It means gathering friends to brainstorm solutions for a local issue.

Or maybe it's as simple as sharing your personal story you never know who it will resonate with and inspire you to action.

I challenge you to start with one action. It could be one of the actionable steps from this book that resonated with you, or something entirely different that fits your mission. Just one action, today or this week.

Invite others to get involved because as we've learned, magic multiplies when it's not just you. And finally, let your purpose provide guidance for the journey. When in doubt or when obstacles arise (and they will), reconnect with your why.

The reason you embarked on this path. That purpose will be your compass, your fuel, and your solace.

In the end, heartfelt fundraising is not really about money, though funds are the means; it's about love in action. It's about channeling our love for our friends, family, neighbors, and even strangers we may never meet, into something that makes their lives better. It's love that motivated the race volunteer to perform CPR.

It's love that inspires a community to donate and volunteer.

And it's love that will continue to light the way forward for all of us who choose to make a difference.

Thank you for reading my story and allowing me to share what I've learned. I look forward to hearing about your story, the one you will write with your actions and impact. Lead Your Heartfelt Fundraising Journey.

Start with one action. Invite others. Let purpose guide your ask, your community, and the world will be better for it, and so will you.

The world needs your heart and your leadership.